STATE V. PEYTON

Second Edition

STATE V. PEYTON

Second Edition

Elizabeth I. Boals

Associate Director
Stephen S. Weinstein Trial Advocacy Program
Washington College of Law
American University

NATIONAL INSTITUTE FOR TRIAL ADVOCACY

Address inquiries to:
Reprint Permission
National Institute for Trial Advocacy
1685 38th Street, Suite 200
Boulder, CO 80301-2735
Phone: (800) 225-6482
Fax: (720) 890-7069
E-mail: permissions@nita.org

ISBN 978-1-60156-597-6
eISBN 978-1-60156-598-3
FBA 1597

Printed in the United States of America

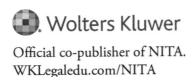

Official co-publisher of NITA.
WKLegaledu.com/NITA

CONTENTS

ACKNOWLEDGMENTS

The author would like to acknowledge The Honorable Michael D. Mason of the Circuit Court for Montgomery County, Maryland, for his insightful suggestions on this publication. The author also acknowledges the special contributions by American University Washington College of Law (WCL) students, Trina Leo and Janissia Orgill, for assisting with editing and creating exhibits for this second edition of the case file and teacher's manual. Thanks also to Kim Green, Program Coordinator for the WCL Trial Advocacy Program, and Mary Ippolito, Senior Administrative Assistant, for their careful editing.

The National Institute for Trial Advocacy wishes to thank Twitter for its permission to use likenesses of its website as part of these teaching materials.

INTRODUCTION

This case file contains materials for the trial of a defendant on the charges of driving under the influence of intoxicants and felonious hit and run. These materials are designed to provide opportunities for users of this case file to consider criminal trial issues, including medical expert testimony, character evidence, criminal conviction impeachment, bias impeachment, prior recorded testimony, and evidence in the form of an audio recorded 911 call and breath test computer printout.

The author hopes that this case file will familiarize attorneys with the many challenges that are an integral part of the preparation and presentation of a criminal case in modern courts of law.

CASE SUMMARY

A grand jury charged Jordan Peyton with driving under the influence of intoxicants and felony hit and run for failing to stop at the scene after she allegedly struck an occupied parked car, causing property damage and personal injury.

At the time of the incident, Peyton was thirty-four years old, five-feet, nine-inches tall, and weighed 175 pounds. She is a founding partner at the architecture firm of Peyton & Dalton, Inc., in Nita City, Nita. On May 15, YR-1, Peyton attended a social event after work. The event was held at the Sunset Bar & Grill. Peyton drove herself and a firm intern, Riley Cameron, to the event.

According to Peyton, she consumed two twelve-ounce bottles of beer at the event between 5:30 and 7:30 p.m. She claims that she did not have any other alcohol that day. Also according to Peyton, Cameron had approximately five twelve-ounce bottles of beer during his two hours at the event. Peyton gave Cameron a ride home from the event.

At approximately 7:35 p.m. on May 15, YR-1, Taylor Addison, a carpenter, was sitting in her Chevy Trailblazer parked along the curb on Second Avenue facing the intersection of Second Avenue and North Market Street. She was holding a cup of extremely hot coffee. Addison took the lid off the cup to let it cool down. Addison was looking down at some papers when she sensed a car pull up on her left. Without warning, Addison's car jerked to the right. The coffee sloshed over the rim of the cup and severely burned her left hand. Addison frantically grabbed for napkins from the passenger seat to soak up the spilled coffee. She looked up and saw a silver or white Mercedes driving slowly on North Market away from the intersection. Addison honked her horn. She saw that the Mercedes had a company sign on the passenger door that said "Peyton & Dalton." As soon as she got the coffee spill under control, she called 911 from her cell phone.

Officer Lee Baldwin arrived on the scene and took Addison's statement. Using the computer in his cruiser, Officer Baldwin ran an internet search on local businesses named "Peyton & Dalton." Only one local business had that name. He cross-referenced the list of employees from the company's website with Department of Motor Vehicles records. A silver Mercedes was registered to one of the firm's partners, Jordan Peyton, at an address just a few miles from the scene. Officer Baldwin drove to Peyton's address, where he saw a silver Mercedes, with a magnetic sign that read "Peyton & Dalton" affixed to the passenger side door, in the process of parallel parking on the street in front of Peyton's house. Officer Baldwin approached the car and spoke briefly to Peyton. He determined that she had been driving through the intersection of Second Avenue and North Market Street approximately thirty minutes earlier. Peyton denied hitting Addison's car. Officer Baldwin observed some scratches on the passenger side of Peyton's car that appeared to him to be consistent with the scratches on Addison's Trailblazer.

During Officer Baldwin's conversation with Peyton, he smelled a slight odor of alcohol coming from her breath and observed that her eyes were glassy and bloodshot. Peyton admitted to having two beers over a two-hour time period earlier that evening. Officer Baldwin asked Peyton to perform three field sobriety tests. In Officer Baldwin's opinion, Peyton's admission to drinking, physical appearance, and performance on the field sobriety tests indicated that she was driving under the influence of alcohol.

Officer Baldwin placed Peyton under arrest for driving under the influence of intoxicants and felony hit and run. During a search incident to formal arrest, Officer Baldwin found a credit card receipt in Peyton's blazer pocket from the Sunset Bar & Grill, dated that same evening. Peyton was very upset and demanded that her blood alcohol content level (BAC) be tested. Officer Baldwin transported her to the police station and brought her into the DUI processing center. At 9:30 p.m., Officer Baldwin administered the BAC exam on an Intoxilyzer. The reading was 0.06. In Nita, BAC must be 0.08 or more for the prosecution to obtain a presumption that the individual was driving under the influence of alcohol.

The applicable law is contained in the statutes and proposed jury instructions set forth at the end of this case file.

All years in these materials are stated in the following form:

1) YR-0 indicates the actual year in which the case is being tried (i.e., the present year);

2) YR-1 indicates the next preceding year (please use the actual year);

3) YR-2 indicates the second preceding year (please use the actual year), etc.

Color copies of the exhibits, and the audio of the 911 telephone call are available online at:

http://bit.ly/1P20Jea
Password: Peyton2

INSTRUCTIONS

Unless otherwise instructed, a party need not call all of the witnesses on their list. All witnesses are gender neutral and can be played by either a man or a woman. Witnesses may not deny that they made a prior statement that is contained in their signed statement or prior testimony. Jordan Peyton may be called only in her own defense.

Version I

    State: Officer Lee Baldwin

                   Taylor Addison

    Defense: Jordan Peyton

                   Riley Cameron

Version II   *Opening:* (handwritten)

    State: Officer Lee Baldwin

                   Taylor Addison

                   Doctor Kipper Williams

    Defense: Jordan Peyton

                   Riley Cameron

                   Doctor Fran Montgomery

Opening!

REQUIRED STIPULATIONS

1) The parties agree that the Intoxilyzer machine used to test Jordan Peyton's blood alcohol content on May 15, YR-1, was properly calibrated and in good working condition.

2) The parties agree that, according to the laboratory tests, the paint samples taken from Taylor Addison's car and Jordan Peyton's car contained only paint consistent with the car from which the scrapings were collected. There was no evidence of paint transfers on either car.

3) The parties agree that the certified criminal record and driving record for Jordan Peyton are accurate and authentic. These certified copies, if relevant and otherwise admissible, shall be admitted without the testimony of the custodian of these records pursuant to Nita Criminal Code § 10-101.

4) The parties agree that the 911 emergency call recording, provided as Exhibit 1, is an accurate and complete recording of the entire 911 call placed by Taylor Addison on May 15, YR-1, at 7:38 p.m. The parties further stipulate that the transcript of this 911 call, provided in Exhibit 2, is an accurate and complete transcription.

5) The defense made motions to suppress, on Fourth and Fifth Amendment grounds: (1) the Sunset Bar & Grill receipt found in Jordan Peyton's blazer pocket when she was searched pursuant to her arrest; (2) Jordan Peyton's oral statements to Officer Baldwin during her stop and arrest; and (3) the May 16, YR-1 written statement made by Jordan Peyton. On these grounds, the court denied the motions.

Case Materials and Exhibits

IN THE CIRCUIT COURT FOR
THE CITY OF NITA

THE PEOPLE OF THE STATE OF NITA	)))	
v.	))	Case No. CR 1112
JORDAN PEYTON	))	
Defendant.	))	

INDICTMENT

The Grand Jury in and for the City of Nita, State of Nita, upon its oath and in the name and by the authority of the State of Nita, does hereby charge the following offenses under the Criminal Code of the State of Nita:

COUNT I

That on May 15, YR-1, within the City of Nita in the State of Nita, JORDAN PEYTON committed the crime of

FELONIOUS HIT AND RUN

in violation of Section 4-101 of the Nita Criminal Code of YR-27 as amended, in that JORDAN PEYTON was the driver of a motor vehicle involved in an accident in which a person was injured or an occupied vehicle was damaged and did not immediately stop as close to the scene of the accident as possible and report personal information as required under Section 4-101.

COUNT II

That on May 15, YR-1, within the City of Nita in the State of Nita, JORDAN PEYTON committed the crime of

DRIVING UNDER THE INFLUENCE OF INTOXICANTS

in violation of Section 6-101 of the Nita Criminal Code of YR-27, as amended, in that JORDAN PEYTON drove or operated a motor vehicle while under the influence of alcohol, which impaired JORDAN PEYTON'S ability to drive or operate a motor vehicle safely.

EXHIBIT 1

AUDIO RECORDING OF ADDISON 911 CALL

Audio of the 911 telephone call is available online at:

http://bit.ly/1P20Jea
Password: Peyton2

Exhibit 2

Transcript of Addison 911 Call

Date: May 15, YR-1
Time: 7:38 p.m.
Caller: Taylor Addison

Police Department Dispatcher (PDD): 911, what's your emergency?

Caller: AHHHH! Some car just hit my car and took off! My hand is really hurt!

PDD: Slow down. Slow down. What is your name?

Caller: Taylor Addison.

PDD: What happened?

Caller: OK, OK, I was in my car holding a cup of coffee, and this car sideswiped me! I can't stop the burning on my hand!

PDD: Can you give me any details about this car or the driver?

Caller: I think it was the Mercedes that hit me. I saw it head down North Market Street. Silver or white with a sign that says "Peyton & Dalton." It must be that architecture firm. I couldn't see the driver. I can't believe this! I just can't believe this.

PDD: OK, do you need any medical assistance?

Caller: Yes.

PDD: I will send a cruiser and ambulance out to you immediately. Where exactly are you?

Caller: I'm at the corner of Second Avenue and, um, North Market Street downtown Nita City. Please hurry up! My hand! Oh, my hand!

PDD: Please stay on the line until emergency assistance arrives.

Caller: Somebody had to see it. Maybe somebody saw the car that hit me. Light colored. Ah, definitely not a truck. A sedan.

Caller: I can hear the sirens. Thanks. Thank you so much.

END OF CALL

[Audio of the 911 telephone call is available online at: http://bit.ly/1P20Jea, Password: Peyton2]

EXHIBIT 3

STATE OF NITA				
POLICE REPORT				

DATE OF INCIDENT OCCURRENCE	TIME	NCIC NUMBER	OFFICER I.D. NUMBER	CASE NUMBER
05-15-YR-1	7:35 p.m.	46768	679	

"X" ONE	"X" ONE	TYPE SUPPLEMENTAL ("X" APPLICABLE)		
[X] NARRATIVE [ ] SUPPLEMENTAL	[X] CRIMINAL REPORT [ ] OTHER	[ ] COLLISION UPDATE [ ] SCHOOL BUS	[ ] FATAL [X] HIT AND RUN [ ] OTHER	

SUBJECT	REPORTING DISTRICT/BEAT	CITATION NUMBER
Arrest of Jordan Peyton	2nd Dist.	N/A

NARRATIVE:

I received a dispatch at 7:38 p.m. reporting a hit and run at the corner of Second Avenue and North Market Street in Nita City. Upon arriving at the scene, I found Taylor Addison sitting on the ground outside of her Trailblazer, which was parallel parked on Second Avenue. I observed her hand was bright red and blistering. While waiting for the ambulance, I took Addison's statement. She told me that she was sitting in her car waiting to meet with a client in a nearby business on a potential job (Addison is a carpenter). She sensed a light-colored car pull up next to her, but she didn't actually look at it because she was reviewing a document. She felt her car jerk to the right. The movement of her car caused her to spill the coffee she was holding. Hot coffee spilled all over her left hand. After spilling the coffee, she tossed the coffee cup out the window and tried to get the coffee off her hand with napkins from the passenger seat. She looked up just in time to see a silver or white Mercedes heading slowly down North Market Street away from the intersection. She saw a sign for the "Peyton & Dalton" architecture firm on the passenger door of the Mercedes. She has worked on projects with this firm so she was familiar with the name. Using the computer in my cruiser, I searched for information on the employees of the Peyton & Dalton architecture firm. The firm's internet site had a list of employees, which I cross-checked with the Department of Motor Vehicles records. A silver Mercedes was registered to one of the firm's partners, Jordan Peyton, at an address a few miles from the scene. There were no other Mercedes registered to Peyton & Dalton employees.

I observed damage to the front driver's side bumper of Addison's Trailblazer. The bumper was not dented, but the paint was scratched. Addison claims there was no previous damage to her bumper.

About this time, the ambulance arrived and the paramedics administered care to Addison. I determined that it was too dark to take quality photographs of the damage. I planned to return to the scene in the morning to collect evidence and take photographs. I proceeded to Jordan Peyton's house.

When I arrived at Peyton's residence, I parallel parked my cruiser at the curb. As I was getting out of my cruiser, I saw a silver Mercedes parallel parking a few cars ahead of me. The driver parked without incident (When the driver got out of the car,) I identified myself and asked her name. She informed me that her name was Jordan Peyton. I asked if she had been the only person driving her car that day; she told me that she had been. I asked her if she had been driving her car through the intersection of Second Avenue and North Market about thirty minutes prior. She said "I think so. I was definitely on North Market. I came up First or Second Avenue to North Market." I shined my flashlight on her car and noticed light-colored scratches on the rear passenger side door panel and wheel well. I asked her about these scratches, and she said the scratches were from an accident in her parking garage at her office. These scratches appeared to me to be consistent with the damage to Addison's vehicle.

Over the course of my conversation with Peyton, I noticed a slight, yet distinct odor of alcohol on her breath. I also noticed that her eyes were glassy and bloodshot. In my experience, both of these observations indicate an individual has consumed alcohol recently. I asked her if she had been drinking that night, and she told me that she "drank two beers earlier that evening." Upon being informed of this, I asked her to perform three field sobriety tests. She agreed.

1. I asked Peyton to stand on one foot with her other foot lifted approximately six (6) inches off the ground in front of her, close her eyes, and slowly count to thirty (30). She asked to remove her shoes and muttered something under her breath about her legs hurting. At her request, I permitted her to remove her shoes. Nevertheless, she was only able to count to six (6) when she had to put her lifted leg down to steady herself. She lifted it again and dropped it again at thirteen (13). She lifted it again, and using her arms for balance, was able to hold it from thirteen (13) to thirty (30), but I already considered her performance on this task a failure and consistent with being under the influence.

2. I asked her to close her eyes, tilt her head back, and put her arms straight out to the sides. Then, I asked her to slowly touch the tip of her index finger to her nose with each hand. She was able to complete this with her right hand on the first attempt. With her left hand, she unsuccessfully attempted to complete this task three (3) times (she overshot her nose each time), but was ultimately able to complete the task on her fourth attempt. She was unsteady on her feet the whole test, although she was able to keep her feet together during the test. I considered her performance on this task a failure and consistent with being under the influence.

3. I asked her to walk heel-to-toe in a straight line for ten (10) steps, turn around, and then walk back heel-to-toe to her original spot. While she was able to walk ten (10) steps forward without deviating from the imaginary line, she had to walk very slowly and use her arms for balance. She could not turn without steadying herself with one foot slightly off to the side. She also stepped off the imaginary line slightly two (2) times on her return trip. She begged to try again because she knew she had performed badly. I denied her request. I considered her performance on this task a failure and consistent with being under the influence.

It should be noted that during the administration of the field sobriety tests Peyton did not seem to take me or the tests seriously. She was condescending and even wanted to use her cellphone during the administration of the tests. She asked me if I "even went to college" and when I responded "Yes, I have a criminal justice degree from Nita College," she laughed and said, "isn't that sweet?"

Based on my ten years as a police officer making DUI arrests and all of the information I had to this point, I placed Peyton under arrest for DUI and felony hit and run and read her the complete Miranda warnings from the police department issued card. During a search incident to her arrest, I found a receipt from the Sunset Bar & Grill from earlier that same evening in her right blazer pocket. I did not ask Peyton any questions about the receipt, but she blurted out, "That's my receipt from the happy hour, but I did not drink all of those drinks." I attached the receipt to this report.

At this point, Peyton became very upset and demanded to have her blood alcohol content (BAC) tested. I was more than happy to comply with her request. Given that I did not have a breathalyzer test in my car, I drove her directly to the DUI processing center at the police station. At 9:32 p.m., Peyton gave a 210 liters breath sample to the Intoxilyzer. She had a reading of 0.06. A copy of the reading was provided to Peyton and is attached to this report.

PREPARER'S NAME, RANK, AND DIVISION	DATE
BALDWIN, LEE, OFFICER, SECOND DISTRICT PATROL	**05-15-YR-1**

EXHIBIT 4

Intoxilyzer—Alcohol Analyzer
Model: 5468-DGI I
Date: May 15, YR-1

Subject Name: Peyton, Jordan

Subject DOB: 10/01/YR-36
Driver Lic. #: 356-88-463OD

Arresting Officer: Baldwin, Lee
Badge #: 679

Testing by: Baldwin, Lee
Testing Time: 9:32 p.m.

Subject Test   0.06 Alcohol Content

EXHIBIT 5

Nita Department of Public Safety

Certifies that on

May 20, YR-2

Officer Lee Baldwin

Successfully completed the certification for the
administration of the Intoxilyzer

_____
Certified Intox. Instructor

_____
Secretary of Transportation

Valid 1 year from Completion Date

EXHIBIT 6

Your Neighborhood Bar

Server: Pat Carter
Date: May 15, YR-1
Time: 7:18 p.m.

Order:
7 Imported Bottle Beer
  @ 5.00 . . . . $35.00

Subtotal $35.00
Tax (10%) $03.50
Total $38.50

Card: xxxx xxxx xxxx 2398

          Tip   _____

          Total   _____

Jordan Peyton

Thank you and come again soon!

customer copy

STATEMENT OF JORDAN PEYTON

My name is Jordan Peyton, and I am thirty-four years old, five-feet, nine-inches tall, and weigh approximately 175 pounds. I reside at 1313 Randolph Road in Nita City. I am not married, and I have no children. I make this written statement freely and voluntarily and without reservation. I waive my rights to remain silent and have an attorney present during questioning. I have been in jail all night, and before I am released I want to tell my side of the story. I am a founding partner at the cutting-edge architecture firm of Peyton & Dalton. I started this firm with a few of my classmates after my graduation from Nita College with a bachelor's degree in Architectural Design. I graduated first in my class in YR-11. The firm is comprised of five partners and fifteen associates. We also employ approximately ten college interns.

I am best known for my work on commercial building designs. My designs have been featured in numerous magazines and architectural books. My commercial projects are often massive in scale and detail.

On Friday, May 15, YR-1, I was planning to attend a firm social event, basically a happy hour from 5:30 to 7:30 p.m., at the Sunset Bar & Grill. Everyone calls it the Sunset. As I am one of the most well-known members of the firm, it is important for me to make an appearance at these events to encourage camaraderie and morale in the firm.

I left the office on May 15 at around 5:15 or 5:20 p.m. and drove down to the Sunset. I gave one of the college interns, Riley Cameron, a ride to the event. There was a pretty good turnout for this particular event, and maybe twenty to twenty-five people were there when we arrived. At the event, I socialized with my coworkers, clients, and some of the Sunset patrons. I did not eat anything while at the Sunset because I had eaten a big lunch. I am also training for a marathon in the fall and trying to stay away from bar food.

That being said, over the course of my time at the Sunset, I had two beers. I also paid for Riley's beers. Riley had been working very hard on the A. T. Moore, Inc., project. Earlier that day, the CEO of A. T. Moore had approved our plans for a new office building. I bought Riley's beers as a thank you for his hard work on this project. I bought beers directly from the bartender and put the beers on the bar tab that I opened with my credit card. As I said, I only had two beers and the rest of the beers on that tab were purchased for Riley.

I was exhausted that evening and eager to be home. I started that day with an early five-mile run. I spent the morning attending back-to-back meetings and, finally, spent all afternoon correcting mistakes associates had made on some of my projects. It was a long and tedious day. By 7:15 p.m., I had been going for more than thirteen hours.

I offered to give Riley a ride to his apartment. I have given him rides home in the past when we work late. He lives between the firm and my house and not far from the Sunset, so it was no trouble. The shortest route to Riley's apartment is up First or Second Avenue, then down North Market and left on Eighth Avenue. Riley lives one block off of Eighth Avenue on Arrow Road.

I had no reservations about driving. I did not feel drunk or even buzzed. It was about an eight-minute drive from the Sunset to Riley's place, and in that time we talked about the A. T. Moore project. During our conversation, Riley did not slur his words or act intoxicated. Riley is a hard worker, but not the brightest student intern. I will not be offering him an associate job when he graduates next month.

The drive through town was bumpy but uneventful. I think I came up First Avenue, took a right on North Market Street, a left on Eighth Avenue, and a right on Arrow Road to Riley's apartment. I don't always take the same route, but I am fairly sure that is the route I took last night. Driving through that part of downtown is tough because of all of the potholes along the side streets and down North Market Street. I stopped at every stop sign and red traffic light that I encountered on the drive. I did not hear a horn honk during this trip, nor did I hit another car. Riley and I talked for a minute outside of his house, and then I drove directly home.

I pulled up to my house and parallel parked in a tight spot right in front. As I was getting out of my car, a police officer approached me and asked me for my name and who had been driving my car that night. I was cooperative. I told him my name and said that I was the only person who drove my car that night. He asked me about some scratches that were on the side of my car. I told him that I park in the garage at work and that I rubbed against the rubbery part of a garage pylon a few days earlier. I had looked at the damage in the dark garage, and it didn't look like much. I figured I would get it buffed out next time I took my car into the shop. As I don't get in on the passenger side of my car, I just forgot about it.

The officer then asked me if I had been drinking. I told him the truth. I told him that I had two beers at my firm's happy hour. Even though I was cooperative and clearly not intoxicated, he made me perform some sobriety tests. He seemed to be on a power trip. He was very curt with me during the whole exchange. My cellphone rang during the tests. The officer went nuts. He yelled at me to turn it off. I had no intention of answering the call, but the officer still got angry.

First, he had me stand on one foot, close my eyes, and count to thirty. I asked him to let me take my loafers off because they are slick on the bottom and I didn't want to perform badly because of my shoes. Also my legs and feet were killing me after my long day. When I started the first test, my legs began to really hurt. He reluctantly allowed me to remove my shoes, but when I started the first test, my legs began to really hurt. Like I said, I am training for the Nita City marathon next fall, and I ran fifteen miles the day before and five miles that morning. I had to drop my foot around number six or seven, but I made it to thirty from there. I only dropped my leg because I was sore from training. I told the officer about my training, but he didn't seem to care.

Next, the officer had me close my eyes, put my head up, and touch my nose with my index fingers. I was perfect on my first attempt with my right index finger, but I had some trouble with my left hand. I am right-handed, so I missed with my left hand a couple times. I finally got it on the third or fourth try with my left hand. I did not stumble or lose my balance during this test. I just missed my nose with my left hand.

Finally, he asked me to walk heel-to-toe in a straight line, turn around, and walk the same way back to my original place. I did fine on this test. I only wobbled slightly on the turn and may have stepped out of line once, just slightly, on the return trip. The officer never told me how fast to do this test, but he made some comment about it "taking long enough." I asked to do it again if he wanted it faster, but he refused.

The officer then told me that he was arresting me for DUI and hit and run. I was shocked. I did not know what he was talking about. I swore to him that I did not hit anyone. He told me that I had sideswiped someone, causing slight damage to the side of some woman's car and causing the woman to injure her hand. I told the officer that I would have stopped if I had sideswiped a car, no matter how slight the damage. He told me the woman identified my car by the "Peyton & Dalton" sign on the door. I had these magnetic P&D logo signs made for the members of the firm to place on their cars. I sent an email last month about them to all of the associates. I wonder if the woman identified my car because I'm a deep pocket to sue. I am going to remove that sign as soon as I get home. If the woman saw this happen, then the only explanation I have is that I did not know that I hit her and possibly I thought I had gone over a pothole or some uneven pavement. I would never knowingly leave the scene of an accident, and I definitely was not drunk.

The officer brought me to the station. While I readily admit that I had two beers at the Sunset, there was no way I was drunk when I was driving. I insisted that the officer give me a breath test to check my blood alcohol content. As I expected, it was only 0.06, which is below the legal limit.

He said that he was still charging me with DUI and hit and run and that I could tell the judge all of my excuses. I can tell this is going to be just like that last time I dealt with the police. When I was in college, I was in a restaurant and left in a hurry because I was ill. I thought the person I was with was going to pay the bill, but he skipped out on the check. I told the police and the court the truth, but I ended up with a misdemeanor conviction.

I could tell that Officer Baldwin just wanted his quota of arrests and didn't care about the truth. This was especially true after he found the Sunset receipt in my pocket. I told him that the seven drinks I paid for were not all for me, but I could tell he didn't believe me.

Signed and attested to this 16th day of May YR-1.

EXHIBIT 7

RE: New advertising strategy

From: outlook_9776ec576c1ad123@outlook.nita on behalf of
        Jordan Peyton (peyton@pandd.nita)
Sent: 5 April YR-1, 9:32:52 AM
To: associates@pandd.com (associates@pandd.nita)
Cc: dalton@pandd.com (dalton@pandd.nita)

1 attachment
Mercedes with decal.docx (452.3 KB)

Dear All Peyton & Dalton Associates,

As you know from our last staff meeting, we are bumping up our marketing and PR efforts to try and attract new clients and get the firm's name out around Nita City. Please stop by my office at your convenience to pick up one of the magnetic P&D logo stickers that we have had made. The logo should be placed somewhere conspicuous on your vehicle so it is clearly visible to pedestrians and other drivers. Please see the attached photo as an example.

Thanks team!

Jordan Peyton, C.E.O
Peyton & Dalton, P.C.
Architectural Designs

EXHIBIT 8

PHOTOGRAPH OF PEYTON & DALTON SIGNAGE

PEYTON & DALTON
Archetectual Designs

"Let's Build Some Dreams Together!"

Exhibit 9

Nita Department of Motor Vehicles	
Driver's Name: Jordan Peyton	DOB: 10/01/YR-36

Driving Record Abstract
As of 01/01/YR-0

Incident Date	Description	Disposition
7/4/YR-3	Charged: Reckless Driving	9/1/YR-3: Reduced – Pled G to Speeding 10–14 MPH over limit

This signature and seal is to certify that this is an accurate copy of the Driving Record of Jordan Peyton as of the date indicated above and that all information contained within this report is true.

DMV Clerk

EXHIBIT 10

Circuit Court of the City of Nita, State of Nita

Defendant's Name: Jordan Peyton	DOB: 10/01/YR-36

Criminal Record
As of 01/01/YR-0

Incident Date	Charge	Disposition
6/1/YR-12	Nita Criminal Code § 22-111 Larceny Under $300 (misdemeanor)	8/4/YR-12: Pled NG/Found G Petit Larceny Sentenced thirty days jail/all suspended—conditioned on uniform good behavior for one year

This signature and seal is to certify that this is an accurate copy of the entire Criminal Record of Jordan Peyton on file at the Circuit Court of the City of Nita, and that all information contained within this report is true.

Susan Johnston

Clerk of the Court

EXHIBIT 11

STATE OF NITA				
POLICE REPORT				
DATE OF INCIDENT OCCURRENCE	TIME	NCIC NUMBER	OFFICER I.D. NUMBER	CASE NUMBER
05-15-YR-1	**7:35 p.m.**	**46768**	**679**	

"X" ONE	"X" ONE	TYPE SUPPLEMENTAL ("X" APPLICABLE)		
☐ NARRATIVE ☐ X	☒ CRIMINAL REPORT ☐ OTHER	☐ COLLISION UPDATE ☐ SCHOOL BUS	☐ FATAL ☒ HIT AND RUN ☐ OTHER	

SUBJECT	REPORTING DISTRICT/BEAT	CITATION NUMBER
Arrest of Jordan Peyton	2nd Dist.	N/A

NARRATIVE:

This is a supplemental report.

At the end of my twelve-hour shift on May 16, YR-1 at approximately 7:00 a.m., I photographed Taylor Addison's silver Trailblazer. When I arrived at the intersection of Second Avenue and North Market Street, the vehicle was in the same position it had been the evening before. As the victim had been transported to the hospital by ambulance, her vehicle appeared to have remained undisturbed all night. The window was even in the down position as it had been the evening before. The paper coffee cup was no longer on the scene. I photographed the vehicle from multiple angles. Photographs are attached to this report.

I collected paint scrapings from the point of impact on the victim's vehicle and secured them in an evidence envelope. On close observation, I could see that the black plastic of the bumper could be seen through the paint in places. I did not observe any paint color other than silver.

On May 16, YR-1, at approximately 7:00 p.m., I proceeded to the residence of Jordan Peyton. Her silver Mercedes was not where it had been parked the night before. I was unable to locate her vehicle on that day. A few days later, I located her vehicle in the parking garage of her office building. The Peyton & Dalton magnetic sign had been removed from the passenger side door. Pursuant to the search warrant I had obtained, I photographed the damage to her vehicle and collected paint scrapings from the scratched area. I secured the scrapings in an evidence envelope. On close observation, I could see what I believed to be black rubber transfer marks that could have come from either the black rubber strip on the base of Addison's front bumper or possibly the black strip on the side of Addison's vehicle. I did not observe any paint color other than silver. Photographs are attached to this report.

Attached is a close-to-scale diagram of the intersection of Second Avenue and North Market Street. I observed a number of potholes, fist-sized dislodged chunks of pavement, and generally poor road conditions on Second Avenue in the blocks directly east of North Market Street; however, there are no potholes or debris within fifteen (15) feet of the location of Addison's vehicle. I reported the poor road conditions to the Nita Department of Transportation.

Tests on the paint scrapings were inconclusive. No affirmative match could be made between the two vehicles. According to the lab, the scrapings from both vehicles appeared to contain only paint consistent with the car from which the scrapings were collected.

PREPARER'S NAME, RANK, AND DIVISION	DATE
BALDWIN, LEE, OFFICER, SECOND DISTRICT PATROL	**05-25-YR-1**

EXHIBIT 12

PEYTON VEHICLE REGISTRATION

NITA Department of Motor Vehicles

Driver's Name: Jordan Peyton	DOB: 10/01/YR-36

Vehicle Registration
As of 01/01/YR-0

Make	Model	Year	License Tag #
Mercedes-Benz	E350/4 door	YR-2	PNDRGR8

This signature and seal is to certify that this is an accurate copy of the Vehicle Registration Information of Jordan Peyton as of the date indicted above and that all information contained within this report is true.

Jim Smithfield
DMV Clerk

EXHIBIT 13

SEARCH WARRANT & INVENTORY SHEET

THE CIRCUIT COURT FOR THE CITY OF NITA

In the Matter of the Search of,   )
the silver Mercedes Benz belonging to   )
Jordan Peyton, residing at   )   Case No. CR 1112
1313 Randolph Road   )
Nita City, 12345   )

SEARCH AND SEIZURE WARRANT

To: Any authorized law enforcement officer

An application by a law enforcement officer or an attorney for the government requests the search of the following property located in the City of Nita:

The YR-2 silver Mercedes-Benz C-Class series 4-door sedan belonging to Jordan Peyton of 1313 Randolph Road, Nita City, 12345, specifically, to collect paint samples from the vehicles for further testing and analysis in a driving under the influence and hit and run investigation.

I find that the affidavit(s), or any recorded testimony, establish probable cause to search and seize the property described above, and that such search will reveal:

That Peyton's Mercedes struck the Victim's Chevy Trailblazer; the paint samples should match paint samples taken from the damaged area of the Victim's Chevy Trailblazer because either the paint from the Victim's vehicle transferred onto Peyton's vehicle or the paint from Peyton's vehicle transferred onto the Victim's vehicle during the collision.

YOU ARE COMMANDED to execute this warrant on or before **May 30, YR 1** *(not to exceed 14 days)*

X in the daytime 6:00 a.m. to 10:00 p.m.   ☐ at any time in the day or night because good cause has been established.

Unless delayed notice is authorized below, you must give a copy of the warrant and a receipt for the property taken to the person from whom, or from whose premises, the property was taken, or leave the copy and receipt at the place where the property was taken.

The officer executing this warrant, or an officer present during the execution of the warrant, must prepare an inventory as required by law and promptly return this warrant and inventory to authorizing judge.

Date and time issued: _____May 15, YR-1_____   _____*Carla Rubin*_____
                                                                          Judge's Signature

City and State: _____Nita City, Nita_____   _____Carla Rubin, Circuit Court Judge_____
                                                                     Printed name and official title

Return

Case No.:	Date and time warrant executed:	Copy of warrant and inventory left with:
CP-1112	5/16/YR1 7:00 PM	

Inventory made in the presence of:

Inventory of the property taken and name of any person(s) seized:

Paint scrapings from the scratched area, rear end of the passenger side, of Jordan Peyton's silver Mercedes with plate number ___PNDRGR8___ .

Certification

I declare under penalty of perjury that this inventory is correct and was returned along with the original warrant to the designated judge.

Date: *5/16/YR1*

Officer Lee Baldwin
Executing officer's signature

Office Lee Baldwin, Second District Patrol
Printed name and title

Exhibit 14

EXHIBIT 15

PHOTOGRAPH OF ADDISON VEHICLE*
(REAR VIEW 1)

*To view images in color, please visit our digital download site at:
http://bit.ly/1P20Jea
Password: Peyton2

Exhibit 16

**Photograph of Addison Vehicle
(Rear View 2)**

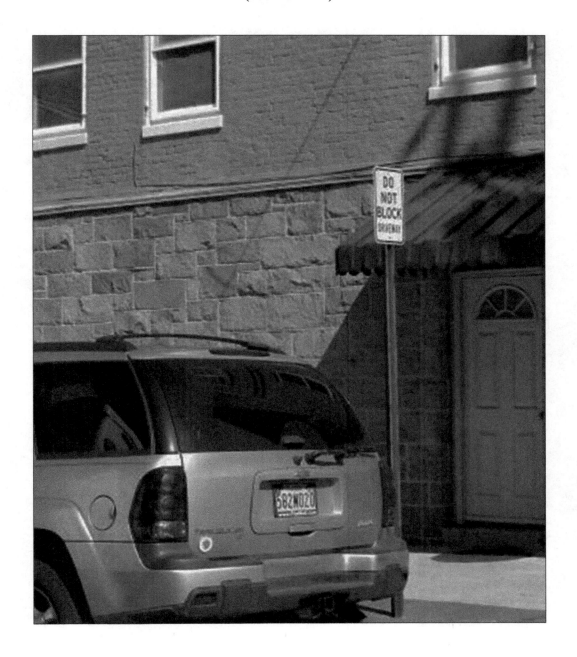

EXHIBIT 17

PHOTOGRAPH OF ADDISON VEHICLE
(DAMAGE)

Exhibit 18

Photograph of Peyton Vehicle
(Damage 1)

Exhibit 19

**Photograph of Peyton Vehicle
(Damage 2)**

STATEMENT OF RILEY CAMERON

Officer Baldwin asked me to write this statement and sign it as a true and accurate account of what happened during my ride home from the happy hour on May 15, YR-1. My name is Riley Cameron. I am twenty-one years old. I live on Arrow Road in Nita City, and I am an intern at the architecture firm of Peyton & Dalton. I go to Nita State University and am in my final year studying architecture. I started working at Peyton & Dalton in May of YR-2 and hope to be hired as an associate after my graduation next month.

During my time as an intern, I have participated in a number of social outings with members of the firm. There would often be alcohol consumed at these events, though I cannot remember an instance in which Ms. Peyton or anyone was drunk or disorderly. At these functions, Ms. Peyton would have a drink or two, at the most, and sometimes she would buy me a few drinks or a meal. She is a very generous person.

On Friday, May 15, YR-1, Ms. Peyton received good news that A. T. Moore, Inc., a real estate development company and one of our big clients, approved our design plans for a large office building in downtown Nita City. I worked on these plans with Ms. Peyton for months. At around 5:00 p.m. that evening, Ms. Peyton came to my cubicle and gave me the news in person. She offered to buy me a few drinks at the firm happy hour that evening as a way of thanking me for my hard work on the plans.

Ms. Peyton and I rode together to the firm happy hour at the Sunset. We arrived around 5:30 or 5:45 p.m. I spent most of my time by the end of the bar, talking with a group of interns. During the course of the event, Ms. Peyton bought me a few beers as a thank you for my work on the A. T. Moore project. I do not remember specifically how many she bought me, but I think it was four. I also ordered myself a beer and a cheeseburger and fries. I paid the bartender directly in cash for the additional beer and food. I think I had maybe five beers total at the event. I certainly wasn't drunk. Five beers really do not have much of an effect on me. I am a college student, so I socialize and drink a lot of beer. Plus, I ate a big cheeseburger and fries that really diluted the effect of the alcohol.

Around 7:20 p.m., Ms. Peyton offered to give me a ride home. I had plans for later that night and I do not have a car, so I accepted her offer.

I know that Ms. Peyton has been charged with DUI. Ms. Peyton was not drunk or even buzzed when she was driving me home. We had a normal conversation about the A. T. Moore project, and she was not slurring her words. The trip from the Sunset to my apartment probably took about five to ten minutes, though I really cannot remember exactly. The trip was routine. I do not remember anything unusual happening. I am not sure which route through downtown she took, but I remember commenting on the need for road repair because it was a bumpy ride.

Officer Baldwin showed me the tweet that I sent out right when I got home on May 15, YR-1. Yes, I wrote that tweet. When I said, "home safely—barely," I was referring to the fact that Ms. Peyton is known for driving fast and riding up on other cars' bumpers. I was just making a joke. She wasn't driving erratically or fast that night. The #hotrod is a running joke between the associates.

Ms. Peyton called me into her office a few days after the happy hour and told me that she had been charged with hitting a car in the intersection of Second Avenue and North Market Street on the way to my place. There is no way she could have hit a car without me knowing it. I don't think we were even on Second Avenue. It is worth noting, I remember seeing scratches on the passenger side of her car when I got in her car to leave the happy hour.

There must be some kind of mistake. Ms. Peyton would never leave the scene of a crime. She is the most honest person I know. Everyone at the firm and people in the architecture community know that Ms. Peyton is honest—almost to a fault—because she tells clients exactly what they can expect in project costs rather than underestimating costs like the rest of the firms in the industry. An associate at the firm told me that Ms. Peyton has lost lucrative jobs because she was too honest with prospective clients.

Signed and attested to this 20th day of May YR-1.

EXHIBIT 20

RILEY CAMERON TWEET

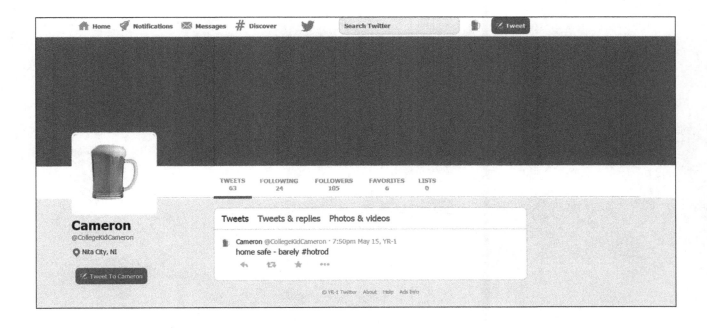

IN THE CIRCUIT COURT FOR
THE CITY OF NITA

THE PEOPLE OF   )
THE STATE OF NITA   )
)
)
v.   )   Case No. CR 1112
)
JORDAN PEYTON   )
)
Defendant.   )

FELONY HIT AND RUN
PRELIMINARY HEARING TRANSCRIPT

Witness: Taylor Addison

Direct Examination by State's Counsel:

1 Q: Please state your name for the record.

2 A: Taylor Addison.

3 Q: What is your address?

4 A: 447 Lockney Drive, Jamesburg, in the State of Columbia.

5 Q: What is your occupation?

6 A: I used to be a carpenter, but I have been out of work since Ms. Peyton hit my car.

7 Defense: I object to Ms. Addison's representation that Ms. Peyton hit her car. I do not

8   believe that Ms. Addison is able to identify the driver of the car that hit her.

9   I object to her characterization.

10 Judge: Overruled. You can explore that issue on cross-examination.

1 Q: Let's talk about the incident. When did it occur?

2 A: May 15, YR-1.

3 Q: Where did it occur?

4 A: At the intersection of Second Avenue and North Market Street. I was parked along the
5 curb in the last space on Second Avenue before that intersection.

6 Q: What happened?

7 A: I was early for a meeting with a potential client, who was planning some storefront ren-
8 ovations. He wanted me to come by at 8:00 p.m., so I got a cup of black coffee and an apple
9 pie from the drive-thru a few blocks from the client's store. That was at about 7:30 p.m.
10 I parked my car on the side of Second Avenue, took off my seat belt, and ate my apple pie.
11 The coffee was extremely hot, so I took off the lid to let it cool. At approximately 7:35 p.m.,
12 I picked up the coffee in my left hand and looked down at some papers in my lap.

13 Q: What happened next?

14 A: I sensed a light-colored car moving past me on my left. I didn't think anything of it
15 until, all of a sudden, my car lurched to the right. The steaming hot coffee sloshed over
16 the rim of the cup and poured over my left hand. I threw the cup out my open car win-
17 dow. I was in so much pain. I grabbed some napkins from the passenger seat and tried to
18 get the coffee off my hand. Once I got the spill under control, I looked up and saw a silver
19 Mercedes heading slowly down North Market Street away from the scene. I think the
20 Mercedes slowed down to stop at the light, hit my car, and then got the green and turned
21 on North Market.

22 Q: What else could you see?

23 A: I saw two people in the Mercedes. I couldn't see the driver's face because she was already
24 on North Market heading north when I was finally able to focus on her through the pain.

1 Defense: I object to Ms. Addison's representation that a woman was driving the Mer-
2 cedes. She just testified that she could not see the driver's face. I object to
3 her characterization.

4 Judge: Sustained. Ms. Addison, please refrain from testifying to things that you do
5 not have firsthand knowledge of.

6 Q: What happened next?

7 A: I beeped my horn a few times with my right hand, but the Mercedes did not stop.

8 Q: Were there any unique characteristics about this Mercedes?

9 A: Yes. It has a sign on the passenger side door for the architecture firm of Peyton &
10 Dalton.

11 Q: What happened next?

12 A: Well, as soon as the Mercedes drove away, I called 911 to report the hit and run. Officer
13 Baldwin arrived within a minute.

14 Q: What did Officer Baldwin do when he arrived?

15 A: He interviewed me.

16 Q: What kind of car were you driving that day?

17 A: A silver Chevy Trailblazer.

18 Q: Was there any damage to your front left bumper before the incident you just described?

19 A: No. The bumper was is perfect shape before Ms. Peyton hit me.

20 Defense: I renew my objection to Ms. Addison's speculation that Ms. Peyton was the
21 driver of the car that hit her.

1 Judge: Sustained. Ms. Addison, please do not make me instruct you again to refrain

2   from testifying to things that you do not have firsthand knowledge of.

3 Q: What did the bumper look like after the incident?

4 A: There were a bunch of scratches on the front driver's side corner of the bumper.

5 Q: After the incident, did you have to bring your car in for repairs?

6 A: Yes, I did. I took the car to the Johnson Brothers. I have known them for a while and know

7 that they are pretty honest guys, so that is where I always bring my car if it needs to be fixed.

8 Q: And did they give you a receipt for the repair work?

9 A: Yes, they did.

10 Q: How much did it cost to fix your bumper?

11 A: The total cost was $480.

12 Q: Ms. Addison, you testified earlier that when the coffee spilled it burned your hand. Can

13 you tell the judge about your injury?

14 A: Yes. I suffered first- and second-degree burns on my left hand and wrist. The coffee was

15 so hot it caused my hand to swell and the skin to turn a deep red and blister in spots. It

16 was extremely painful.

17 Q: Ms. Addison, I am showing you a photograph that has been marked as State's

18 Exhibit 21. Can you tell the judge what is depicted in this photograph?

19 A: Yes, this is a photograph that was taken by the medical staff in the emergency room

20 where I was admitted on the evening of May 15, YR-1. That is exactly what my hand and

21 wrist looked like within an hour or so of the coffee spill.

22 Q: I move to admit State's Exhibit 21 in evidence.

1   Judge: Admitted.

2   Q: Have you healed from the injury?

3   A: Mostly, but the new skin on my hand is still sensitive to the sun and hot and cold tem-
4   peratures. Since I am left-handed, my injury is constantly coming in touch with things
5   and each touch sends a slight ting of pain up the back of my hand.

6   Q: Did the driver of the silver Mercedes stop and talk to you after hitting your car?

7   A: No.

8   Q: I have nothing further.

9   **Cross-Examination by Defense Counsel:**

10   Q: Your car was parked on Second Avenue?

11   A: Yes.

12   Q: Second Avenue is a one-way street with two lanes?

13   A: Yes.

14   Q: Your car was parked on the right side of the street facing North Market Street?

15   A: Yes.

16   Q: In the area around where you parked, there are signs on the sides of Second Avenue
17   that indicate the parking regulations in that area?

18   A: I think so.

19   Q: In fact, there were signs right next to where you parked your car?

20   A: I think so.

1   Q: There was a sign that indicated that only compact cars should park in the space your
2   car was parking in?

3   A: The officer did point that out to me, but said he was not going to give me a citation for it.

4   Q: Your Trailblazer is not a compact car, correct?

5   A: No.

6   Q: You did not see the Mercedes actually strike your car, did you?

7   A: No, but I felt it.

8   Q: You did not see the Mercedes on Second Avenue?

9   A: No, but I felt it hit my car.

10   Q: The Mercedes did not speed away, did it?

11   A: No, but it didn't stop either.

12   Q: The driver did not turn around and look at you?

13   A: No.

14   Q: The passenger did not turn around and look at you?

15   A: No.

16   Q: You did not follow the Mercedes?

17   A: No. I was in shock and pain.

18   Q: After you got the burn under control and looked up, the Mercedes was actually on
19   North Market, correct?

20   A: Yes.

1   Q: You didn't see the Mercedes turn from Second to North Market, did you?

2   A: I didn't have to see it. It was evident because the Mercedes was going slowly as if it had

3   just turned on to North Market.

4   Q: And there were other cars on North Market?

5   A: I am not sure.

6   Q: And there were other cars on Second Avenue?

7   A: I don't think so.

8   Q: You know that Peyton & Dalton is a successful residential and commercial architecture

9   firm?

10   A: Yes.

11   Q: And you know that means that the partners in the firm are very wealthy?

12   Prosecutor: Irrelevant.

13   Judge: Sustained.

14   Q: Ms. Addison do you intend to sue Ms. Peyton in civil court for the injuries you received

15   from this accident?

16   A: Absolutely. I plan to sue her after the criminal charges are resolved.

17   Defense: I have nothing further.

I certify that the foregoing document is a true and accurate transcription of Taylor Addison's preliminary hearing testimony, which was given under oath, on July 15, YR-1, in the case of *State v. Jordan Peyton* in the District Court, Nita City, Nita.

Certified by:

John Allan Michael
Court Reporter

Commission number: 6548
My Commission expires: December 30, YR-0

EXHIBIT 21

PHOTOGRAPHS OF ADDISON HAND INJURY*

*To view images in color, please visit our digital download site at:
http://bit.ly/1P20Jea
Password: Peyton2

Exhibit 22

Johnson Brothers Auto Collision Experts

"It's broken—so fix it"

Damage Description:	
Front driver's side bumper scratched	**Date: 05/19/YR-1**
Repair Description:	**Time: 3:30 PM**
Replaced front bumper	

Repair Detail:

Parts	
New Front Bumper	$350
Labor ($100/hour)	
1 hour	$100
Subtotal:	$450
Sales Tax:	$30
Total:	**$480**

IN THE CIRCUIT COURT
FOR THE CITY OF NITA

THE PEOPLE OF THE STATE OF NITA	)	
	)	
	)	
v.	)	Case No. CR 1112
	)	
JORDAN PEYTON	)	
	)	
Defendant.	)	

FELONY HIT AND RUN
PRELIMINARY HEARING TRANSCRIPT

Witness: Pat Carter

Direct Examination by State's Counsel:

1   Q: Please state your name, address, and occupation for the record.

2   A: My name is Pat Carter. I live at 335 Sylvan Lake Road in Nita City. I am currently an

3   assistant manager and bartender at the Sunset Bar & Grill.

4   Q: How long have you worked at the Sunset Bar & Grill?

5   A: Ten years.

6   Q: And is there any training associated with your positions?

7   A: Yes. I have a bachelor degree from Southern Nita University in Hotel and Restaurant

8   Management, and I have taken courses on bartending and bar management.

9   Q: What did you learn in your bartending and bar management courses?

10   A: Well, I learned how to mix drinks and deal with customers. I also learned how to spot

11   and deal with intoxicated individuals, as well as all of the business procedures for run-

12   ning a restaurant and bar.

1   Q: Why is it important to learn how to spot and deal with intoxicated patrons?

2   A: Well, you need to know when to stop serving them for their own safety and the safety

3   and enjoyment of the other patrons.

4   Q: What are the signs that someone is intoxicated?

5   A: Intoxicated people slur their words, have glassy and bloodshot eyes, are unsteady on

6   their feet, and often have trouble following simple instructions such as "you need to leave

7   the bar now."

8   Q: What types of things are involved with running the bar at Sunset?

9   A: Well, on nights that I work, I am responsible for handling the nightly receipts.

10   Q: What do you mean by "receipts"?

11   A: Receipts are the printouts of how the patrons' orders were paid. For example, a receipt

12   will show what was ordered and if the person paid cash or credit. If a person paid by

13   credit, it will show the name, order, date, amount paid, and the last four digits of the

14   credit card.

15   Q: How are the credit card receipts handled?

16   A: I collect all of the credit card receipts at the end of the night and make a notation on

17   the balance sheets. Then I collect the money and put it in the safe for the night. I have to

18   make sure we were paid for everything we served, so the total of credit card sales and

19   cash should equal the amount sold that night.

20   Q: How long do you keep the credit card receipts?

21   A: Two years, as required by state law.

22   Q: Where are they kept?

23   A: In the office file cabinet.

1   Q: Why do you keep the receipts?

2   A: Well, it's company policy to keep them for at least two years to properly report them

3   for business purposes and also to settle any disputed charges that may arise with credit

4   card companies or patrons.

5   Q: Did you review anything before testifying here?

6   A: Yes, I looked at the receipts from May 15, YR-1.

7   Q: Why May 15, YR-1?

8   A: Because you asked me to.

9   Q: Did you work at the Sunset on May 15, YR-1?

10   A: Yes.

11   Q: How do you remember that you worked that day?

12   A: Easy. It was my birthday. I was scheduled to have the night off, but Peyton & Dalton had

13   a social event scheduled and the other two bartenders were unavailable. I wasn't happy

14   about being there, but I was there.

15   Q: Let the record reflect that I am showing defense counsel what has been marked as

16   State's Exhibit 23. Your Honor, may I approach the witness?

17   Judge: Yes, you may.

18   Q: Mr. Carter, can you identify State's Exhibit 23?

19   A: Yes. It is Jordan Peyton's bar receipt from May 15, YR-1.

20   Q: How do you know what it is?

21   A: It has the Sunset logo on the top and contains the date, her name, and my name as the

22   server.

1   Q: Is this one of the receipts you were referring to earlier in your testimony?

2   A: Yes. This is a credit card receipt from May 15, YR-1. I collected it with all of the other

3   receipts from that night and retained it in our files for tax and credit card purchase veri-

4   fication purposes.

5   Q: Is that your regular business procedure?

6   A: Yes.

7   Q: Has this document been modified in any way since May 15, YR-1?

8   A: No. It is the original.

9   Prosecutor: Your Honor, I move for admission of State's Exhibit 23 into evidence.

10   Defense: I object to this receipt on the grounds that there is a double layer of hear-

11   say. Although it appears to satisfy the business records exception, it still

12   contains notations apparently made by a computer system regarding the

13   number of beers ordered and paid for on this receipt. There is no way for

14   the defendant to cross-examine the computer to ensure the reliability of

15   this information.

16   Judge: Objection overruled. The receipt is admitted.

17   Q: What information is contained on the receipt?

18   A: The Sunset logo, date of May 15, YR-1, and Jordan Peyton's name, signature, and the last

19   four digits of the credit card number of the card she used. The receipt also has my name

20   listed as the server. It shows that she paid for seven imported bottled beers that night, and

21   she paid sometime after the receipt was printed at 7:18 p.m.

22   Q: Who is Jordan Peyton?

23   A: She is the boss over at Peyton & Dalton.

1   Q: How do you know her?

2   A: She comes into the Sunset four or five times a month. Sometimes she is alone, and

3   other times with friends. She also comes when Peyton & Dalton has events.

4   Q: Was she present at the social event on May 15, YR-1?

5   A: Yes.

6   Q: Do you personally recall if she was drinking?

7   A: Yes, I remember serving her some beers.

8   Q: How many beers did you give her?

9   A: Well, she ordered seven beers, so I served her seven.

10   Prosecutor: No further questions.

11   **Cross-Examination by Defense Counsel:**

12   Q: You stated she ordered seven beers; did you see her drink any of them?

13   A: Well, not exactly. The bar was pretty packed, so I didn't see her actually drink any of

14   the beers.

15   Q: As a matter of fact, it is common practice for people to buy drinks for other people,

16   isn't that correct?

17   A: Yes, that's a pretty common thing to do.

18   Q: Ms. Peyton did not slur her words on May 15, did she?

19   A: Not that I recall.

20   Q: She did not have trouble walking to or from the bar?

1   A: Not that I recall.

2   Q: Never appeared intoxicated at all, in fact?

3   A: Not that I recall.

4   Q: You did not prohibit Ms. Peyton from ordering alcohol on May 15, YR-1, did you?

5   A: No.

6   Q: You never cut her off?

7   A: No.

8   Q: You did not cut anyone off on May 15, YR-1, did you?

9   A: I don't remember.

10   Q: Mr. Carter, do you know Riley Cameron?

11   Prosecution: Objection. Outside the scope.

12   Judge: Sustained.

I certify that the foregoing document is a true and accurate transcription of Pat Carter's preliminary hearing testimony, which was given under oath, on July 15, YR-1, in the case of *State v. Jordan Peyton* in the District Court, Nita City, Nita.

Certified by:

John Allan Michael

John Allan Michael
Court Reporter

Commission number: 6548
My Commission expires: December 30, YR-0

EXHIBIT 23

Your Neighborhood Bar

Server: Pat Carter Date:
May 15, YR-1
Time: 7:18 p.m.

Order:
7 Imported Bottle Beer
@ 5.00 . . . . $35.00

Subtotal $35.00
Tax (10%) $03.50
Total $38.50

Card: xxxx xxxx xxxx 2398

Tip   6.00

Total   44.50

Jordan Peyton

Thank you and come again soon!

merchant copy

EXHIBIT **24**

STATE OF NITA	*Page 1 of 1*
POLICE REPORT	

DATE OF INCIDENT OCCURRENCE	TIME	NCIC NUMBER	OFFICER I.D. NUMBER	CASE NUMBER
05-15-YR-1	**7:35 p.m.**	**46768**	**679**	**CR-1112**

"X" ONE	"X" ONE	TYPE SUPPLEMENTAL ("X" APPLICABLE)		
☐ NARRATIVE ☒ SUPPLEMENTAL	☒ CRIMINAL REPORT ☐ OTHER	☐ COLLISION UPDATE ☐ SCHOOL BUS	☐ FATAL ☒ HIT AND RUN ☐ OTHER	

SUBJECT	REPORTING DISTRICT/BEAT	CITATION NUMBER
Arrest of Jordan Peyton	**2nd Dist.**	**N/A**

NARRATIVE:

This is a supplemental report.

On July 25, YR-1, Pat Carter was killed in a fire at the Sunset Bar & Grill. News article is attached to this report.

On August 1, YR-1, I contacted the receptionist at Peyton & Dalton to check the status of Riley Cameron's employment with the firm. The receptionist stated that Mr. Cameron was not hired as an associate of the firm in June YR-1. She volunteered that after Mr. Cameron was let go from Peyton & Dalton in the summer of YR-1, he took an associate position with the competing architecture firm of Caston Architectural Designs.

PREPARER'S NAME, RANK, AND DIVISION	DATE
BALDWIN, LEE, OFFICER, SECOND DISTRICT PATROL	**08-01-YR-1**

Exhibit 25

July 26, YR-1

NITA CITY POST
Arson Suspected Cause of Sunset Bar & Grill Fire

By: Jane Dabber

The Sunset Bar & Grill, 1301 Brentwood Road in Nita City, was set ablaze after closing time last night, according to investigators. The Nita City Fire Department now suspects the fire to be the result of an arsonist.

The Sunset Bar & Grill was completely destroyed in the blaze. Nothing was salvable, including all of the furniture, inventory, and business records. During an interview, the owner of Sunset Bar & Grill sadly stated, "This is a tragic occurrence, and although I have considered it, I do not plan on rebuilding the Sunset Bar & Grill."

The tragic fire not only annihilated the restaurant, but it took two lives. One has been identified as Pat Carter, 34, assistant manager and long-time bartender of the Sunset Bar & Grill. The second victim has yet to be identified. The owner addressed his sorrow for the loss of a well-respected and hard-working employee, "Pat will be greatly missed and remembered for his exceptional customer service and kind smile." The Nita City Police Department continues to investigate the fire, as there are no suspects yet. If you have any information on this fire, please contact the Nita City Police Department.

Exhibit 26

MEMORANDUM

To: Office of the State's Attorney

From: Law Offices of Defense Counsel

Date: June 20, YR-1

Enclosed is a close-to-scale diagram, drafted by my paralegal, illustrating the route Ms. Peyton took from the Sunset, up First Avenue, and on to the passenger's apartment. Also enclosed are two photographs as examples of the poor road conditions on First Avenue one block west of North Market Street and two photographs as examples of the poor road conditions on Second Avenue one block west of North Market Street. Ms. Peyton took these photographs.

In the interest of an efficient resolution of this case at trial, we provide these potential trial exhibits in advance of trial.

EXHIBIT 27

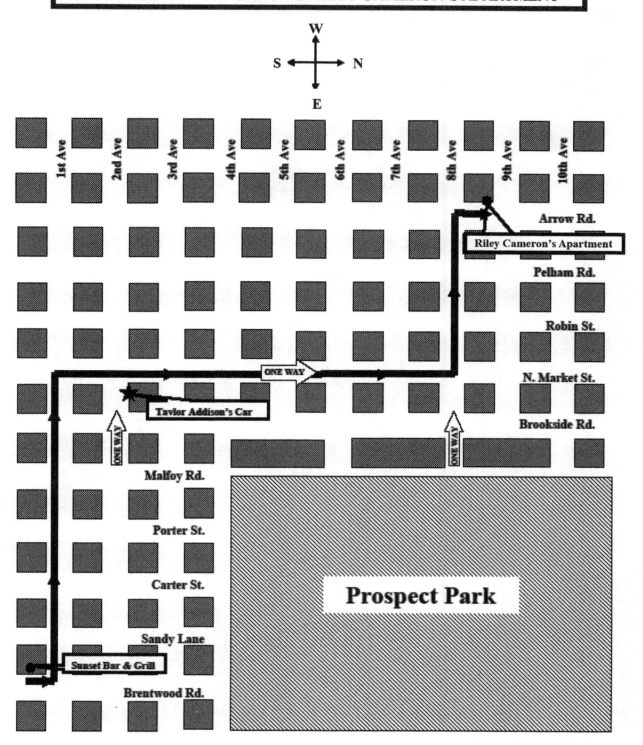

MAP FROM SUNSET GRILL TO RILEY CAMERON'S APARTMENT

Exhibit 28

Map from Sunset Grill (without route and signage)

EXHIBIT 29

POTHOLE ON FIRST AVENUE ONE BLOCK EAST OF NORTH MARKET STREET*

*To view images in color, please visit our digital download site at:
http://bit.ly/1P20Jea
Password: Peyton2

EXHIBIT 30

POTHOLE ON FIRST AVENUE ONE BLOCK EAST OF NORTH MARKET STREET

EXHIBIT 31

POTHOLE ON SECOND AVENUE ONE BLOCK EAST OF NORTH MARKET STREET

EXHIBIT 32

POTHOLE ON SECOND AVENUE ONE BLOCK EAST OF NORTH MARKET STREET

EXPERT WITNESS TESTIMONY

KIPPER WILLIAMS, MD

Nita State University Hospital

2187 University Avenue

Nita City, Nita 81287

Phone: 719-555-3827 Fax 719-555-1138 Email kwilliams@nsuh.nita

---

August 20, YR-1

Re: Jordan Peyton Driving Under the Influence and Hit and Run

Dear Assistant State's Attorney:

Per your request, I have reviewed the Jordan Peyton police case file and Intoxilyzer test results to determine the likely BAC of Ms. Peyton at the time she struck the victim's car. In my expert opinion and to a reasonable degree of medical certainty, Ms. Peyton's BAC was likely between 0.09 and 0.11 at the time of the incident.

Introduction

As we have never worked together on a case, I have attached my CV for your reference. As you can see from my CV, I am uniquely qualified to analyze cases such as this one. I am presently a resident physician at Nita State University Hospital. Last year, I received my MD from Xavier University School of Medicine in Aruba. I earned a BS in Criminal Justice from Nita University. After graduating from college, I attended the Nita State Police Academy and then worked as a state trooper for six years. During my years on the force, I was certified to administer blood alcohol tests using the Intoxilyzer. During my last few years as a state trooper, I was certified as an instructor to teach other officers the proper procedures for administrating Intoxilyzer tests. As a state trooper, I administered hundreds of Intoxilyzer tests and testified in approximately eighty DUI cases as a witness police officer for the State.

I have consulted with the State on a number of DUI cases since my graduation from medical school, but the defendants in those cases pled guilty, so I was not required to testify in court. I have never assisted a defendant in a DUI case or testified in court as a medical expert.

Blood Alcohol Content

On average, it takes approximately one hour for the average human body to metabolize one alcoholic drink. In this context, one drink equals a five-ounce glass of wine, twelve-ounce beer, or one-and-a-half ounce shot of liquor.

According to the police report, the defendant stated that she consumed two beers between 5:30 and 7:30 p.m. and had not eaten anything since lunch. An empty stomach will speed up the alcohol absorption rate. This means that Ms. Peyton's BAC would reach its peak more quickly than it would have if she had a full stomach. I have attached a bell curve diagram to generally illustrate this process.

To a reasonable degree of medical certainty, I believe that Ms. Peyton was near the peak of her BAC at the time she was driving and down the decreasing side on the bell curve when she submitted her sample to the Intoxilyzer. Extrapolating backward from the time of her test, I would say that her BAC at the time she was driving was between 0.09 and 0.11.

In addition, it is highly unlikely that the defendant is telling the truth about the amount of alcohol she consumed. By the time she was given the Intoxilyzer test, approximately two and a half hours had passed since her last drink of alcohol. There is no possible way that she could have had only two beers between 5:30 and 7:30 p.m. and still register a 0.06 at 9:30 p.m.

It is highly likely that the defendant consumed four to six beers at the event. This conclusion is supported by the officer's observations of the defendant outside her residence approximately thirty minutes after consuming her last drink. As reported by the officer, Ms. Peyton had glassy and bloodshot eyes. Consumption of two beers over a two-hour period is not likely to manifest itself in glassy and bloodshot eyes; however, consumption of four to six beers in that time period would likely have that effect. The officer's observations of Ms. Peyton during the field sobriety tests also support the conclusion that Ms. Peyton was under the influence of alcohol to a degree consistent with her consumption of four to six beers rather than two beers as she claimed.

Conclusion

As I have stated above, I believe that Ms. Peyton had a BAC between 0.09 and 0.11 when she was driving on May 15, YR-1. At a BAC in this range, Ms. Peyton's motor skills, vision, and judgment would be impaired to a degree that would make it unsafe for her to operate a motor vehicle. In fact, medical studies have shown that any BAC above 0.08 would likely indicate that she was impaired to the point that she could not operate a motor vehicle safely.

I hope this information assists with your successful prosecution of Ms. Peyton. If I can help further, please do not hesitate to contact me. As I told you on the phone, I will not charge the State for my services in this case as I feel it is my civic duty.

Sincerely,

Kipper Williams, MD

BELL CURVE CHART ACCORDING TO DR. KIPPER WILLIAMS

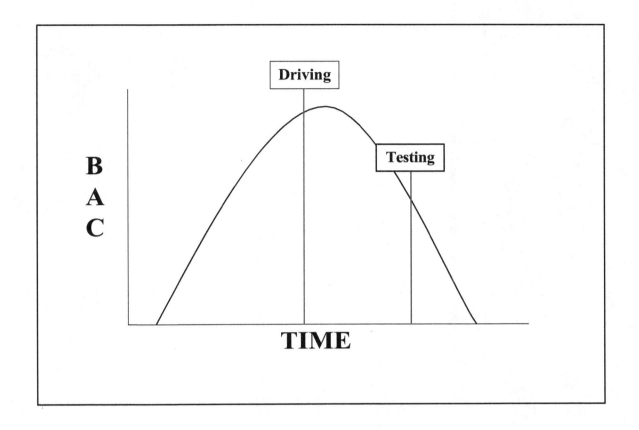

KIPPER WILLIAMS, MD
CURRICULUM VITAE

EDUCATION

YR-5 to YR-1   Xavier University School of Medicine, Aruba
Doctor of Medicine

YR-8 to YR-5   Nita State University (night program)
Bachelor of Science, Biology

YR-11 to YR-10   Nita State Police Academy

YR-15 to YR-11   Nita State University
- Bachelor of Science, Criminal Justice
- President of MADD chapter

PROFESSIONAL EXPERIENCE

YR-1 to present   Residency: Nita State Hospital

YR-11 to YR-5   Nita State Police
- State Trooper
- Certified DUI Testing Instructor

PROFESSIONAL ORGANIZATIONS

- Lifetime Member, Nita State Police Officers' Organization
- National Association Against Drunk Driving

PUBLICATIONS

"Blood Alcohol Content and Driver Impairment," *Nita Journal of Medicine*, YR-3. An in-depth examination of the relationship between BAC and driver impairment.

"Drunk Driving Enforcement Begins at Home," *MADD Annual Newsletter*, December YR-6.
An article that serves as a practical guide to family intervention in the behaviors that lead to driving under the influence.

"Community Policing of Drunk Driving," *Nita Times Dispatch*, March 20, YR-10.
An article suggesting that community groups, local governments, and educators have a critical role to play in the fight against drunk driving.

MEMORANDUM

TO: Counsel for Jordan Peyton

FROM: Fran Montgomery, MD, PhD

DATE: October 20, YR-1

RE: *State v. Jordan Peyton*

Per our agreement, I have reviewed the police report, Intoxilyzer test results, and Kipper Williams's analysis of the Peyton case. I have formulated an opinion as to the accuracy of Dr. Williams's conclusion that Peyton likely had a blood alcohol content (BAC) of between 0.09 and 0.11 and was operating her vehicle under the influence of alcohol at the time of the incident. I believe that Dr. Williams's analysis is faulty and that without consideration for Peyton's physiological attributes and other environmental factors, and without a BAC test taken closer to the time of driving, it is not possible to conclude within a reasonable degree of medical certainty that Peyton had a BAC higher than 0.06 or was impaired at the time she was driving.

Background and Agreement

You have agreed to compensate me at a rate of $200 per hour for my analysis and report drafting and $400 per hour for my in-court testimony. I have attached my CV for your reference. In addition to my traditional credentials, in YR-1 I was the recipient of the B. C. Woodward Foundation Grant for research in the area of the abuse of forensic evidence in legal proceedings. This is a $200,000 grant over the course of three years. I am researching decided legal cases that relied heavily on questionable scientific evidence. The goal of my research is to highlight the impact of science on legal proceedings and support stricter ethical rules governing the testimony of medical professionals at legal proceedings. All of my fees from this case will be invested in this research project.

In addition, I have never testified for the State on this or any other issue. If I am called to testify in this case, it will be the fifth time I have testified in court as an expert on this issue.

General Information

I have a particular interest in the use of BAC as evidence in DUI prosecutions. This is an area of concern to me because I believe courts rely too heavily on BAC as a determining factor in assessing impairment. There is no reliable science linking a particular individual's actual impairment with a generic BAC level. I have treated many intoxicated patients during my time in the emergency room, and I have witnessed individuals with the same BAC demonstrate vastly different degrees of impairment. Factors such as body weight, stomach contents, environmental contaminants such as gas fumes or cigarette smoke, and the presence of medications or fever in the body can all dramatically impact the BAC reading and the level of impairment between individuals with the same BAC.

Case-Specific Analysis

According to Peyton, she consumed two beers within a two-hour period on a relatively empty stomach. Peyton was also training for a marathon, which leads me to believe she may have a great deal of lean muscle mass and a low body fat percentage. Lean muscle contains more water, which absorbs alcohol from the bloodstream and works to lower BAC. A body with lean muscle mass can tolerate more alcohol than a body with little muscle mass, because a body with more lean muscle mass processes alcohol more slowly. This means, to use Dr. Williams's bell curve analysis, Peyton would move more slowly along the bell curve than an individual with less muscle mass. In addition, a person with more lean muscle mass may demonstrate less impairment than a person with high body fat content. This only scratches the surface of the physiological factors that should have been, but were not, considered by Dr. Williams.

The more troubling issue with the prosecution's reliance on Peyton's 0.06 BAC as evidence of any level of impairment when she was driving is that she was given the Intoxilyzer test at 9:30 p.m., nearly two hours after she was driving. This passage of time diminishes the reliability of the reading. In his analysis of Peyton's BAC, Dr. Williams assumes that her absorption of alcohol remained constant at all times throughout the alcohol metabolization process. This process does not occur at a uniform pace, with the body processing alcohol at the same rate over time. Rather, this process occurs at differing rates where during some periods more alcohol is processed, while during others, the rate slows down dramatically. Although this process generally resembles a bell curve, it is impossible to say with any high degree of medical probability what Peyton's BAC at an earlier time would have been. Any such opinion is merely a guess based on assumptions and conjecture, not science.

As you have asked me to give my opinion as to Peyton's likely BAC at the time she was driving, in my opinion, the alcohol level in Peyton's body was likely just peaking at the time of the Intoxilyzer test. Therefore, in my expert opinion, her BAC at the time she was driving would have been lower than the 0.06 that she registered when tested. This is consistent with my earlier statement that if Peyton's body had high lean muscle content, her body would process alcohol more slowly. It is also consistent with Peyton's claim that she only had two beers at the earlier event. I have attached my analysis, plotted on Dr. Williams's bell chart, to demonstrate how my position differs from Dr. Williams's position. If compelled to give a likely range of BAC when she was driving, I would estimate it to be between 0.03 and 0.05. Please keep in mind that I do not state this range to a reasonable degree of medical certainty, as that would be impossible after the passage of more than two hours from the time of driving and without a full report of Peyton's physiological attributes and other environment factors.

In my opinion, the Intoxilyzer results from Peyton's test are an unreliable indication of her BAC or her level of impairment during her driving. Dr. Williams's analysis is faulty because it does not take into consideration physiological and environmental factors and relies exclusively on the results of a BAC test performed two hours after the driving. Any extrapolation backward from the time of the test to determine Peyton's likely BAC or level of impairment at the time she was driving would be a mere guess. Further, to use a generic and fairly arbitrary BAC level such at 0.08 as a threshold to conclude that someone is impaired to the point of being unsafe fails to consider numerous factors that have been shown to impact impairment.

BELL CURVE CHART ACCORDING TO DR. FRAN MONTGOMERY

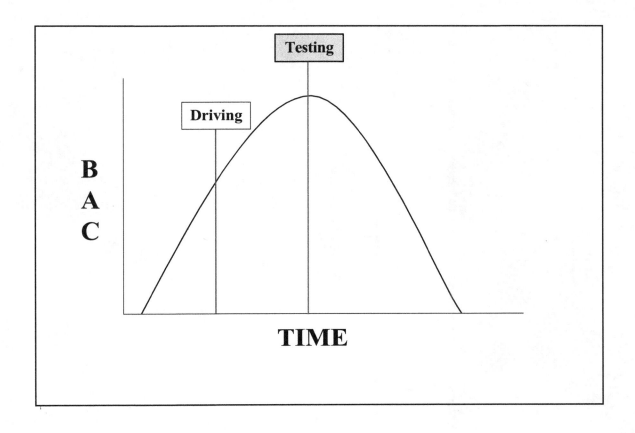

Fran Montgomery, MD, PhD

EDUCATION & PROFESSIONAL EXPERIENCE

YR-1—Present   Attending Physician: Nita City Hospital
- Emergency Department

YR-3—YR-1   Columbia University
- PhD, Forensic Toxicology

YR-7—YR-3   Residency: Duke Hospital
- Internal Medicine

YR-11—YR-7   Duke University School of Medicine
- Doctor of Medicine
- Specialization in Toxicology and Internal Medicine
- Graduated *magna cum laude*

YR-15—YR-11   Duke University
- BS Biochemistry
- Graduated *magna cum laude*

PROFESSIONAL AFFILIATIONS & AWARDS

Recipient, B. C. Woodward Foundation Grant for research in the area of abuse of forensic evidence ($200,000 over three years, beginning YR-1)

Society of Forensic Toxicologists

American Academy of Forensic Sciences

The International Association of Forensic Toxicologists

PUBLICATIONS

"Drunks Rising: The Grey Science of Rising and Failing Curves of Drunkenness," *Legal Times*, December YR-1.
An article on the difficulty of determining blood alcohol content retroactively.

"Science on the Witness Stand," *Journal of Forensic Science*, May YR-2.
An article on the persuasive presentation of scientific information to jurors and lay people.

APPENDICES

NITA STATUTES

Nita Criminal Code—Article 4

Section 4-101. Duty of driver to stop, etc., in event of accident involving injury or death or damage to attended property

The driver of any motor vehicle who is knowingly involved in an accident in which a person is killed or injured, or in which an occupied vehicle is damaged, shall immediately stop as close to the scene of the accident as possible without obstructing traffic and report his or her: (a) name, (b) address, (c) driver's license number, and (d) vehicle registration to the local law-enforcement agency, and to: (a) the person struck or injured if that person seems capable of understanding and retaining the information, (b) if present, some other occupant of the vehicle collided with, or (c) the custodian of the injured property.

The driver shall also render reasonable assistance to any person injured in such accident. "Accident," for purposes of this Article, is defined as any unintentional or intentional contact between a motor vehicle and another motor vehicle, train, person, animal, or inanimate object that results in damage or injury, no matter how slight.

Violation of this section is a felony punishable for up to ten years in prison and/or a $2,500 fine.

Nita Criminal Code—Article 6

Section 6-101. Driving motor vehicle under the influence of intoxicants

It shall be unlawful for any person to operate any motor vehicle on a public roadway while such person is under the influence of alcohol or any other self-administered intoxicant or drug of any nature, or any combination of such drugs to a degree that impairs his ability to drive or operate any motor vehicle safely.

Section 6-201. Implied consent to post-arrest testing to determine drug or alcohol content of blood

Any person, whether licensed by the State of Nita or not, who operates a motor vehicle in the State of Nita shall be deemed thereby, as a condition of such operation, to have consented to have samples of his or her blood, breath, or both blood and breath taken for a chemical test to determine the alcohol and/or drug content of his or her blood, if he or she is arrested for violation of driving a motor vehicle while intoxicated, within two hours of the alleged offense.

Section 6-202. Presumptions from alcohol content of blood

In any prosecution for a violation of § 6-101, the amount of alcohol in the blood of the accused at the time of the alleged offense, as indicated by a chemical analysis of a sample of the accused's blood or breath to determine the alcohol content of his blood, shall give rise to the following rebuttable presumptions:

A. If there was at that time 0.08 percent or more by weight by volume of alcohol in the accused's blood or 0.08 grams or more per 210 liters of the accused's breath, it shall be presumed that the accused was under the influence of alcoholic intoxicants.

B. If there was at that time less than 0.08 percent by weight by volume of alcohol in the accused's blood or less than 0.08 grams per 210 liters of the accused's breath, such fact shall not give rise to any presumption that the accused was or was not under the influence of alcoholic intoxicants, but such fact may be considered with other competent evidence in determining the guilt or innocence of the accused.

Nita Criminal Code—Article 10

Section 10-101. Admissibility of Certified Court and Agency Records

The records of any judicial proceeding and any other official records of a court or State agency, if otherwise admissible, shall be received into evidence without the testimony of the record's custodian, provided that such records are authenticated and certified by the clerk of the court or agency having legal custody of the record.

Section 10-107. Admissibility of Blood Alcohol Content Test Results

Blood Alcohol Content (BAC) test results shall be admissible in a criminal or civil matter as long as the following requirements are satisfied:

A. the test was conducted by a certified administrator for the specific equipment used to test the sample;

B. the administrator's certification was made by a state agency, and a document of certification is available for the court's review; and

C. the equipment was in proper working order at the time of the test.

CASE LAW

State v. Jacobs, 10 Nita 325 (YR-15). A defendant who was seated in a car with the engine off without wearing a seat belt is not guilty of the crime of failing to wear a seat belt. The plain language of the statute suggests that the legislature only intended that seat belts be worn when the car is either "moving or the engine is engaged."

State v. Michaels, 15 Nita 100 (YR-10). This case reaffirmed the specific intent of "knowingly" for the crime of hit and run under Nita Criminal Code Section 4-101. The plain language of the statute suggests that the legislature intended for a defendant to be guilty of this crime only when the defendant "knowingly hit a vehicle and fled the scene." In *Michaels*, the court held that the defendant was not guilty because there was no evidence the defendant knew or should have known that he hit the victim's car.

State v. Daniels, 23 Nita 120 (YR-5). The criminal case law in Nita mandates that in order for a breath test to be admissible using an Intoxilyzer, the test must be given within two hours of the defendant driving the vehicle. In *Daniels*, the defendant was given the test two hours and twenty minutes after driving, and the court held the test results were inadmissible because they were an unreliable indicator of the BAC of the defendant when driving.

INFORMATION ON BURNS

Thermal Burns

Thermal burns are caused by any hot or heated source such as a flame, scald (from steam, hot or molten liquid), or contact (from a hot object, such as a hot cooking pan). While most thermal burns are mild, some may be quite severe. The severity of the burn depends on the number of layers of skin affected. The severity of burns can be either referred to by degrees (first, second, third) or their thickness (superficial, partial, and full).

Types of Burns

First-Degree Burn or Superficial Burn

This burn only affects the epidermis, or the outer layer of the skin. The symptoms of this kind of burn are a painful, red area that turns white when touched. There are not usually blisters.

Second-Degree Burn or Partial Thickness Burn

This burn affects the epidermis and some portions of the dermis, the second layer of the skin. Depending on how much of the dermis is involved, this can be further characterized as superficial or deep.

A superficial partial-thickness burn is painful and red, turning white when touched. There are often blisters and mottling. Hairs are still present.

A deep partial-thickness burn may or may not be painful depending on whether the burn is deep enough to burn the nerve endings. Hair is usually gone from the area of the burn.

Skin Burns

NORMAL SKIN   FIRST DEGREE BURN

SECOND DEGREE BURN   THIRD DEGREE BURN

Third-Degree Burn or Full Thickness Burn

This burn is the most severe kind of burn. It burns all of the epidermis and dermis, and nerve endings, blood vessels, hair follicles, and sweat glands are all destroyed. If the burn is very severe, it may involve bone and muscle. This kind of burn is painless, with no sensation to touch. The appearance is usually pearly white or charred and may appear leathery.

Information on Breath Tests And Intoxilyzer

Why a Breath Test?

Breath testing for alcohol is based upon the principle that alcohol is excreted unchanged in human breath because of equilibrium conditions between lung capillaries and pulmonary alveoli. At constant temperatures, the amount of alcohol in the breath is proportional to the amount of alcohol in the blood.

Method

The process begins when a person breathes into the machine. A quartz lamp then radiates infrared energy, which travels through a chamber that contains the person's breath. After leaving the chamber, a lens focuses the energy into a chopper wheel containing three narrowband infrared filters. The infrared energy passed by the filters is focused on a highly sensitive photodetector that converts the infrared pulses into electrical pulses. The microprocessor interprets the pulses and calculates the BAC that is then displayed.

The Intoxilyzer

The Intoxilyzer, in particular, uses infrared spectrometry to measure alcohol concentration in a breath sample. The instrument measures the degree alcohol absorbs infrared energy; more alcohol present, the greater the absorption.

Operating the Intoxilyzer is simple. A single push of a button controls the entire breath sequence. Further, there is a digital display along with audible tones that guides the operator through the test, preventing any procedural errors. Once the test is complete, test results are printed on a three-part carbonless evidence card.

Proposed Jury Instructions

These instructions are taken from the Nita Model Jury Instructions and reflect the current law of Nita.

1) You have been selected and sworn in as jurors. You must arrive at your verdict by unanimous vote. You must base your verdict on the facts and the law. First, you must determine the facts from the evidence presented in the trial and not from any other source. Second, you must accept and follow the law as I state it to you, regardless of whether you agree with it.

2) The State of Nita has charged the defendant with the crimes of driving under the influence of intoxicants, and felonious hit and run. The defendant has pleaded not guilty.

3) To prove the crime of driving under the influence of intoxicants, the state must prove all the following propositions:

   a. while operating a motor vehicle;

   b. on a public roadway;

   c. the defendant was under the influence of alcohol, or any other self-administered intoxicant or drug of any nature, or any combination of such drugs, to a degree as to impair his/her ability to drive or operate a motor vehicle safely.

If you find from your consideration of all the evidence that each of these propositions has been proved beyond a reasonable doubt, then you should find the defendant guilty of driving under the influence of intoxicants.

If, on the other hand, you find from your consideration of all the evidence that any of these propositions has not been proven beyond a reasonable doubt, then you should find the defendant not guilty of driving under the influence of intoxicants.

4) To prove the crime of felonious hit and run, the state must prove all the following propositions:

   a. while operating a motor vehicle, the defendant knew that he or she was involved in an accident;

   b. as a result of the accident, a person was injured or an occupied vehicle was damaged; and

   c. the defendant failed to stop as close to the scene of the accident as possible without obstructing traffic and report his or her (1) name, (2) address, (3) driver's license number, and (4) vehicle registration to the local law-enforcement agency, and to (1) the person struck or injured if that person seems capable of understanding and retaining the information, (2) if present, some other occupant of the vehicle collided with, or (3) to the custodian of the injured property.

"Accident" for purposes of this case means any unintentional or intentional contact between a motor vehicle and another motor vehicle that results in damage, no matter how slight.

If you find from your consideration of all the evidence that each of these propositions has been proven beyond a reasonable doubt, then you should find the defendant guilty of felonious hit and run.

If, on the other hand, you find from your consideration of all the evidence that any of these propositions has not been proved beyond a reasonable doubt, then you should find the defendant not guilty of felonious hit and run.

Blood Alcohol Content as Evidence of Impairment.

You may consider the amount of alcohol in the defendant's blood at the time of the alleged offense as indicated by a chemical analysis of a sample of the defendant's blood or breath.

If you find that there was, at the time of the offense, 0.08 grams of alcohol or more per 210 liters of the defendant's breath, you shall presume that the defendant was under the influence of alcoholic intoxicants. The defendant may rebut this presumption.

If however, you find that there was, at the time of the offense, less than 0.08 grams of alcohol per 210 liters of the defendant's breath, such fact shall not give rise to any presumption that the defendant was or was not under the influence of alcoholic intoxicants, but such fact may be considered with other competent evidence in determining the guilt or innocence of the defendant.

Direct and Circumstantial Evidence.

The law recognizes two kinds of evidence—direct and circumstantial. Direct evidence proves a fact directly without further need for other evidence. Circumstantial evidence is a fact or circumstance that, if proven, provides a basis for a reasonable inference of another fact or facts.

The law makes no distinction between direct and circumstantial evidence as to the degree or amount of proof required, and each should be considered according to whatever weight or value it may have. All of the evidence, direct and circumstantial, should be considered and evaluated by you in arriving at your verdict.

[Optional Instruction]

Expert Testimony.

You heard testimony in this case from witnesses with special knowledge, skill, experience, training, or education in a particular subject. These types of witnesses are referred to as expert witnesses. In determining what weight to give to the testimony of the expert witnesses, you should consider the qualifications and believability of the witness, the facts upon which each opinion is based, and the reasons for each opinion. You are not bound by the opinion of any expert witness. Give each opinion the weight you find it deserves. You may disregard any opinion if you find it to be unreasonable.

IN THE CIRCUIT COURT FOR THE CITY OF NITA

THE PEOPLE OF THE STATE OF NITA   )
)
         v.   )   Case No. CR 1112
)
JORDAN PEYTON   )
)
Defendant.   )

VERDICT

We, the jury, return the following verdict, and each of us concurs in this verdict: [Choose the appropriate verdict]

1. FELONIOUS HIT AND RUN

On the charge of felonious hit and run, we, the jury, find the defendant, Jordan Peyton:

_____ GUILTY

_____ NOT GUILTY

_____

Presiding Juror

2. DRIVING UNDER THE INFLUENCE OF INTOXICANTS

On the charge of driving under the influence of intoxicants, we, the jury, find the defendant, Jordan Peyton:

_____ GUILTY

_____ NOT GUILTY

_____

Presiding Juror